OVERWATCH®

ANTHOLOGY

VOLUME 1

OVERWATCH®

ANTHOLOGY

VOLUME 1

SCRIPTS BY

Robert Brooks | Matt Burns | Michael Chu
Micky Neilson | Andrew Robinson | James Waugh

ART BY

Bengal | Jeffrey "Chamba" Cruz | Espen Grundetjern
Miki Montlló | Nesskain | Joe Ng | Gray Shuko

LETTERING BY

Richard Starkings and Comicraft's John Roshell,
Jimmy Betancourt, and Albert Deschesne

FRONT COVER ART

Miki Montlló

LICENSED
BLIZZARD
ENTERTAINMENT
PRODUCT

DARK HORSE BOOKS

BLIZZARD CREDITS

Writers: ROBERT BROOKS, MATT BURNS, MICHAEL CHU, MICKY NEILSON, ANDREW ROBINSON, JAMES WAUGH

Art Direction: LOGAN LUBERA

Editors: ROBERT SIMPSON, CATE GARY, ALLISON MONAHAN

Creative Consultation: CHRIS METZEN, JEFF KAPLAN, MICHAEL CHU, ARNOLD TSANG, BILL PETRAS, VALERIE WATROUS

Lore Consultation: SEAN COPELAND, JUSTIN PARKER, EVELYN FREDERICKSEN

Production: TIMOTHY LOUGHRAN, DEREK DUKE, ADAM GERSHOWITZ, CAROLINE HERNÁNDEZ, JOEL TAUBEL, RYAN THOMPSON

Project Manager: BRIANNE M LOFTIS

Senior Manager, Global Licensing: BYRON PARNELL

Director, Creative Development: RALPH SANCHEZ

Special Thanks: DOUG GREGORY, CHARLOTTE RACIOPPO, JEFFREY WONG, RACHEL DE JONG, MICHAEL BYBEE

DARK HORSE CREDITS

Publisher: MIKE RICHARDSON

Collection Editor: DAVE MARSHALL

Collection Assistant Editor: RACHEL ROBERTS

Collection Designers: DAVID NESTELLE and PATRICK SATTERFIELD

Digital Art Technician: ALLYSON HALLER

 Facebook.com/DarkHorseComics

 Twitter.com/DarkHorseComics

Advertising Sales: (503) 905-2537 | International Licensing: (503) 905-2377 | Comic Shop Locator Service: comicshoplocator.com

This volume collects issues #1 through #12 of the digital comics series *Overwatch*, originally published by Blizzard Entertainment.

Published by
Dark Horse Books
A division of
Dark Horse Comics, Inc.
10956 SE Main Street
Milwaukie, OR 97222

DarkHorse.com
Blizzard.com
PlayOverwatch.com

Scholastic edition: January 2018
ISBN 978-1-50670-767-9

10 9 8 7 6 5 4 3 2 1
Printed in Canada

McCREE: *TRAIN HOPPER*

SCRIPT BY ROBERT BROOKS | ART BY BENGAL | LETTERING BY RICHARD STARKINGS
AND Comicraft's JOHN ROSHELL AND JIMMY BETANCOURT

FROM SEA TO SHINING SEA IN EIGHT HOURS WITHOUT LEAVING THE GROUND.

WONDERS NEVER CEASE.

AIN'T THE FASTEST OR THE CHEAPEST WAY TO TRAVEL. BUT THAT'S THE APPEAL.

RICH FOLKS LOVE TO GO WHERE THE GETTIN'S EXPENSIVE.

BUT, HEY, THE FOOD IS GREAT.

SO IS THE BOURBON SELECTION.

NOT THAT I'D KNOW.

THEY DON'T SELL FOLKS LIKE ME A TICKET.

GOOD THING I PREFER THE FRESH AIR.

EVEN IF IT'S BLOWING PAST AT 640 KILOMETERS PER HOUR.

YESSIR. NOTHING LIKE TRAVELING IN STYLE.

UNLESS...

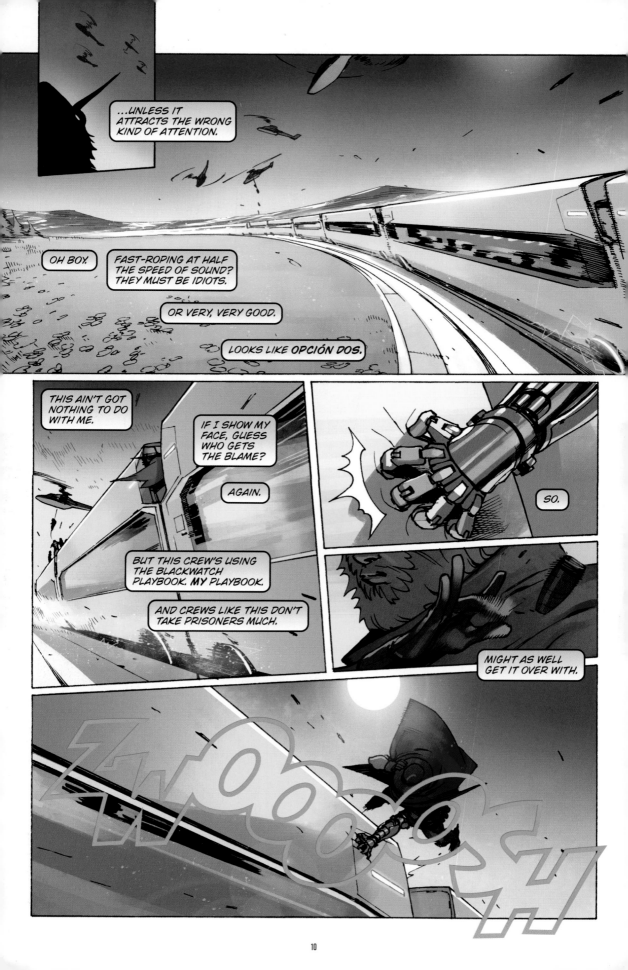

REINHARDT: *DRAGON SLAYER*

SCRIPT BY **MATT BURNS** | ART BY **NESSKAIN** | LETTERING BY **RICHARD STARKINGS**
AND Comicraft's **JOHN ROSHELL** AND **JIMMY BETANCOURT**

MAYBE WE SHOULD SIT THIS ONE OUT. LET SOMEBODY ELSE TAKE CARE OF THINGS FOR ONCE.

AS YOU SAID, THE LOCAL AUTHORITIES HAVE NO POWER HERE ANYMORE.

THERE IS NO ONE ELSE.

KLIK

SHOOM

WE NEED NEW PARTS. YOUR ARMOR CAN'T HANDLE ANOTHER BATTLE IN THIS CONDITION.

WHEN HAS THAT EVER STOPPED US BEFORE? EVEN OLD AND WORN...

"...THIS ARMOR CAN STILL SERVE ITS PURPOSE.

"ONE DAY IT MAY FALL APART. BUT UNTIL THAT TIME, WE WILL *FIGHT*.

"OVERWATCH MAY BE GONE, BUT ITS LEGACY ENDURES THROUGH US. WE HAVE SWORN TO CARRY ON ITS IDEALS AND RESTORE HOPE TO THIS TROUBLED WORLD..."

I'VE LOCATED THE DRAGONS. THEY'RE IN AN OLD FACTORY A FEW KILOMETERS OUTSIDE OF TOWN.

END

JUNKRAT & ROADHOG: *GOING LEGIT*

SCRIPT BY ROBERT BROOKS | ART BY GRAY SHUKO | LETTERING BY RICHARD STARKINGS
AND Comicraft's JOHN ROSHELL AND JIMMY BETANCOURT

KA WHOOOOOM

I'M COMING FOR YA, YA SCRAP-HEADED--!

...OH-THERE'S-NO-TOP-FLOOR-YOU-SONS-OF...

HOOOOOOF

...LEAST IT DIDN'T BREAK THIS TIME... NOW. WHERE ARE YA BASTARDS?

INTRUDER DETECTED.

OI.

OI! THAT WAS MY KILL!

KRSHWING

SYMMETRA: *A BETTER WORLD*

SCRIPT BY ANDREW ROBINSON | ART BY JEFFREY "CHAMBA" CRUZ

LETTERING BY RICHARD STARKINGS

AND Comicraft's JOHN ROSHELL AND JIMMY BETANCOURT

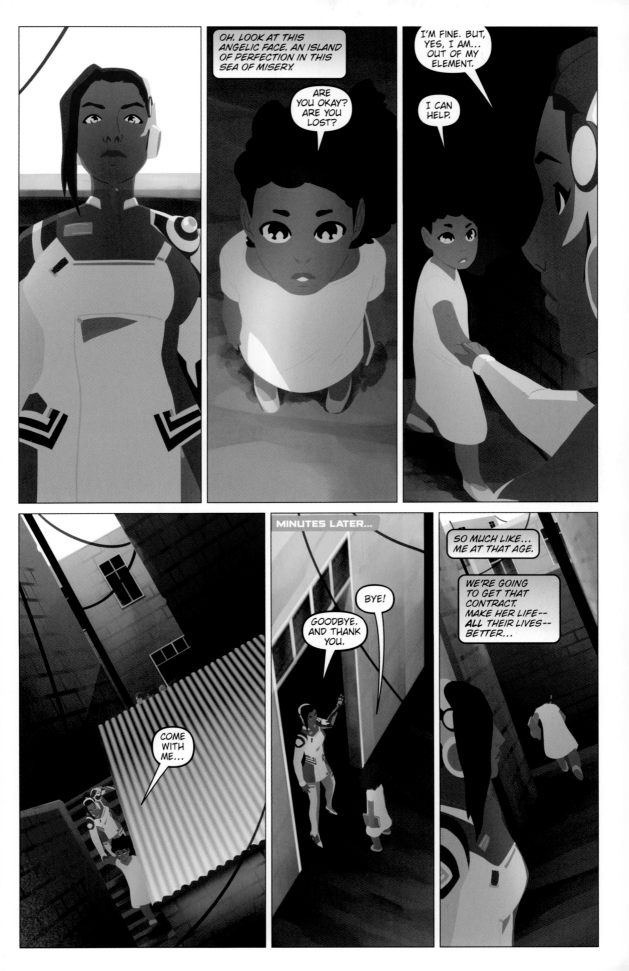

SANJAY? I'M AFRAID THERE'S NOT ENOUGH ON CALADO.

PERHAPS WE CAN GET TO THE MAYOR INSTEAD, FIND SOMETHING ON HER.

THAT IS DISAPPOINTING. BUT SO BE IT.

BAMF

CALADO

KA THOOM

WHAT...?

THERE WERE MEN INSIDE...

WHATEVER DO YOU MEAN?

MY GODS...

CALADO WON'T STAND IN THE WAY OF THE GOOD WE WILL DO IN THIS CITY.

NOT CALADO--THE FAVELA!

ROSA! MEU BEBÊ!*

*MY BABY!

THERE...

I HAVE YOU-- YOU'RE SAFE NOW. I WON'T LET ANYTHING HAPPEN TO YOU.

OH. NO. HER FACE. IT'S...RUINED.

AAYYY! MEU DOCE ANJO...*

MAYBE...MAYBE WE CAN FIX THIS. ALL OF IT...

*MY SWEET ANGEL...

AND SO, AT LONG LAST, DESPITE OCCASIONAL SETBACKS...

...WE ARE PROUD TO OPEN OUR NEW CITY CENTER!

A SHAME ABOUT CALADO'S HOLDINGS...BUT THIS WAS A MOST SATISFACTORY OUTCOME, NO?

THE MAYOR HAD NO CHOICE BUT TO HAVE US STEP IN.

WE WERE GOING TO GIVE THEM HOUSING.

AND WILL THEIR LIVES BE THE BETTER FOR IT?

WE WILL.

WHAT FITS THEIR STATION...AND SERVES THE GREATER ORDER. THAT IS HOW VISHKAR WORKS.

THE FIRE IN THE FAVELA...WAS THAT PART OF THE PLAN?

HOW CAN YOU THINK SUCH A THING?

AND YET... THAT IS THE PRICE OF REBIRTH AND GROWTH. ISN'T IT, SATYA?

YES...OF COURSE.

HE'S RIGHT. WE'RE MAKING THE WORLD A BETTER PLACE...

WE'RE MAKING THE WORLD A BETTER PLACE.

END

PHARAH: MISSION STATEMENT

SCRIPT BY ANDREW ROBINSON | ART BY NESSKAIN | LETTERING BY RICHARD STARKINGS AND Comicraft's JOHN ROSHELL AND JIMMY BETANCOURT

WAS AFRAID THAT SOMEDAY I'D HAVE TO MAKE THIS DECISION.

WHICH IS MORE IMPORTANT...

...THE MAN...

...OR THE MISSION?

FIFTEEN MINUTES EARLIER...

HELIX SECURITY SHOULD HAVE UPGRADED THE ANUBIS FACILITY AFTER WE TOOK IT OVER A FEW YEARS BACK.

AND NOW THE WORST HAS HAPPENED--OR IT'S ABOUT TO.

THE ANUBIS A.I.--ONE OF THE "GOD PROGRAMS" OVERWATCH QUARANTINED AFTER THE OMNIC CRISIS-- BROKE ITS CONTAINMENT AT 2300 HOURS.

THE COMPANY SENT IN AN ENGINEERING TEAM AT 0200 HOURS TO REGAIN CONTROL OF THE COMMAND CENTER. DEAD AIR SINCE.

MOM ALWAYS SAID SHE DREADED THIS PART--WALKING INTO THE UNKNOWN.

BUT IT'S WHAT I ALWAYS LOVE MOST.

CAPTAIN! OVER HERE!

EASY, SON. WHAT HAPPENED?

SO HELIX SENT MY TEAM IN.

WE'RE NOT AN ENGINEERING TEAM. WE'RE A "KILL EVERYTHING" TEAM.

THE SENTRY BOTS... SAID ANUBIS SAW US AS A THREAT, AND THEN THEY STARTED SHOOTING.

THEY SAID **WHAT?**

KKKKKKKKK

<BZZZZZT...>

DID... IT...?

WHRRRrrrrr

WHRRRrrrrr

CL-CLANG

SKRAAAK

GOOD JOB, ROOK--TARIQ.

...GROAN...

SALEH? YOU ALIVE?

...NO...

OH. GUESS I'M NOT BUYING DINNER.

WAIT...MAYBE I'M A LITTLE BIT ALIVE.

LEAN ON ME.

TORBJÖRN: *DESTROYER*

SCRIPT BY MICKY NEILSON | ART BY GRAY SHUKO | LETTERING BY RICHARD STARKINGS
AND Comicraft's JOHN ROSHELL AND JIMMY BETANCOURT

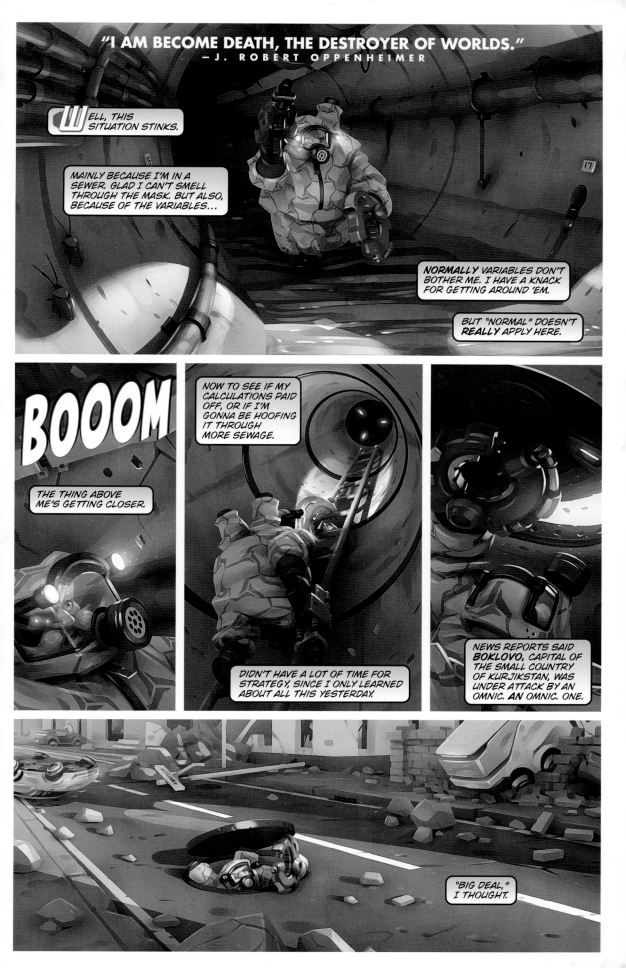

YOU WERE ALWAYS SO GOOD AT *BULLDOZING* THROUGH OBSTACLES.

AND YOU ALWAYS *CHEATED* YOUR WAY PAST THEM. AN ENGINEER SHOULD RESPECT THE PROBLEM, NOT JUST *BYPASS* IT.

THAT'S WHY WE MADE SUCH A *GREAT* TEAM.

CLMP

CLNKT

THNKT

THESE DEFENSES ARE *AUTOMATED.* YOU'RE GONNA GET YOURSELF *KILLED.*

WHY'RE YOU DOING THIS, *SVEN?* WHAT'S THE ANGLE?

MY *ANGLE,* OLD FRIEND, IS THE *PRESERVATION* OF OUR *SPECIES.*

SHNK

RAT·TA·TA·TA

MM-HMM. AND YOU ASKED IF *I* WAS CRAZY?

KURJIKSTAN IS A *CORRUPT DICTATORSHIP* BENT ON EXPANSION...

...ITS METHODS ARE *RUTHLESS* AND *IMMORAL.*

IT IS A *DANGEROUS,* INCREASINGLY *UNPREDICTABLE* PLAYER ON THE *GLOBAL STAGE...*

AND I HAVE JUST *CRUSHED* IT.

THIS CAMPAIGN WAS A *DEMONSTRATION.* MY ULTIMATE WEAPON, IN THE HANDS OF A RESPONSIBLE GOVERNMENT...WILL *SAVE* COUNTLESS LIVES.

AND HOW MUCH WOULD A RESPONSIBLE GOVERNMENT HAVE TO *PAY* FOR THIS PRIVILEGE?

FOR ALL YOUR GRANDSTANDIN' AND PHILOSOPHIZIN', AT THE END OF THE DAY, YOU'RE NOTHING MORE THAN A SLEAZEBAG *PROFITEER!*

SKR-NK

YOU KNOW, WHEN THE OMNICS TOOK OUR TECHNOLOGY AND TWISTED IT TO THEIR NEEDS, IT INFURIATED ME...

BUT AT LEAST I UNDERSTOOD IT.

AARRGGH!!

ANA: *LEGACY*

SCRIPT BY ANDREW ROBINSON | ART BY BENGAL | LETTERING BY RICHARD STARKINGS
AND Comicraft's JOHN ROSHELL, JIMMY BETANCOURT, AND ALBERT DESCHESNE

I'VE DONE THIS JOB PROUDLY SINCE THE OMNIC CRISIS. BUT...I HAVE GROWN WEARY.
I DON'T KNOW HOW MUCH LONGER I HAVE IN ME.
A NEW RECRUIT APPROACHED ME JUST THE OTHER DAY.
HE LOOKED AT MY RIFLE STOCK...ALL THE NOTCHES...
...AND ASKED ME HOW MANY PEOPLE I'VE KILLED.
YOU COULD HEAR THE ADMIRATION IN HIS VOICE.
I'M CONSIDERED ONE OF THE FINEST SNIPERS ON THE PLANET.
MY CYBERNETIC EYE MAKES MY VISION **SIX** TIMES GREATER THAN NORMAL. MY SCOPE BRINGS THAT TO **SIX HUNDRED TIMES**. I RARELY EVEN NEED THE SCOPE.
MY RIFLE IS A KINAMURA. TODAY I'M USING .338 ROUNDS.
ACCURATE TO 2000 METERS. BULLET TRAVELS AT 980 METERS PER SECOND.
I COULD DO WITH LESS. BUT ENEMIES DON'T GET UP FROM THIS.
THE KEY IS TO NOT HESITATE. WHEN YOU HAVE THE SHOT... YOU TAKE THE SHOT.
THAT'S HOW YOU STAY ALIVE. IT'S HOW YOU KEEP YOUR PEOPLE ALIVE.
ALL UNITS, THIS IS MORRISON. WE HAVE THE HOSTAGES. MOVING OUT. ANA, YOU READY?

ANA: *OLD SOLDIERS*

SCRIPT BY MICHAEL CHU | ART BY BENGAL | LETTERING BY RICHARD STARKINGS
AND Comicraft's JOHN ROSHELL, JIMMY BETANCOURT, AND ALBERT DESCHESNE

JUNKENSTEIN

PLOT BY MICHAEL CHU | SCRIPT BY MATT BURNS | ART BY GRAY SHUKO

LETTERING BY RICHARD STARKINGS AND Comicraft's JOHN ROSHELL,
JIMMY BETANCOURT, AND ALBERT DESCHESNE

"IN THE HEART OF THE BLACK FOREST, THERE IS A TOWN CALLED *ADLERSBRUNN*--A TOWN AFFLICTED WITH A TERRIBLE CURSE.

"LONG AGO, IT WAS HOME TO ONE *DR. JAMISON JUNKENSTEIN.*

"HE WAS A BRILLIANT SCIENTIST WHO SERVED THE LOCAL LORD, CRAFTING EXTRAORDINARY, LIFELIKE AUTOMATONS.

"THE LORD WAS A *VERY* HANDSOME AND STATELY RULER, WISE AND JUST, BUT HE HAD NO LOVE FOR THE DOCTOR.

"HE TREATED JUNKENSTEIN'S 'USELESS TRINKETS' AS NOTHING MORE THAN SLAVES.

"THE GOOD DOCTOR COULD ONLY TAKE SO MUCH ABUSE.

"HE WOULD MAKE *TRUE LIFE.*

"HE WOULD EARN THE RESPECT OF THE LORD AND THE TOWNSFOLK BY MAKING A CREATURE THAT COULD THINK FOR ITSELF.

REFLECTIONS

SCRIPT BY MICHAEL CHU | ART BY MIKI MONTLLÓ
LETTERING BY RICHARD STARKINGS AND Comicraft's JOHN ROSHELL,
JIMMY BETANCOURT, AND ALBERT DESCHESNE

FWOOOSH

FWOOOSH

YES! SCORE ONE FOR TRACER!

FWOOOSH

-SIGH-

MISS, THE STORE IS CLOSING. IF YOU DON'T HAVE ANY PURCHASES...

BINARY

SCRIPT BY MATT BURNS, JAMES WAUGH | ART BY JOE NG | COLORS BY ESPEN GRUNDETJERN
LETTERING BY RICHARD STARKINGS AND Comicraft's JOHN ROSHELL,
JIMMY BETANCOURT, AND ALBERT DESCHESNE

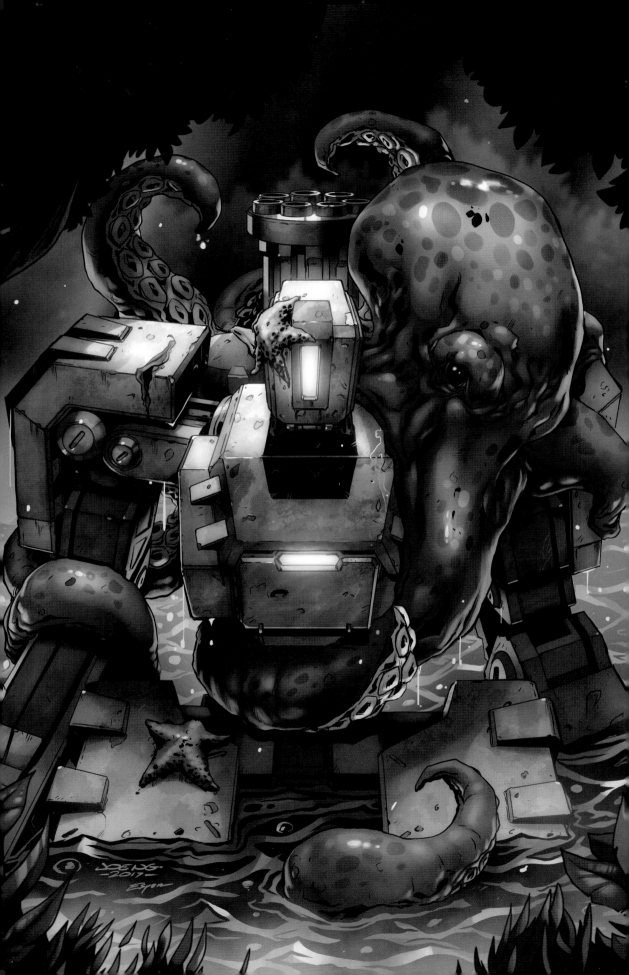

BASTION PÅ RYMMEN? ELLER ÄNNU ETT FALSKT LARM?

*BASTION ON THE LOOSE? OR JUST ANOTHER FALSE ALARM?

FÖRÄLSKADE TONÅRINGAR MÖTER DÖDSMASKIN!

*TEEN LOVERS' RUN-IN WITH DEATH MACHINE!

TIDIGARE TERROR TILLBAKA!

*A TERROR FROM THE PAST RETURNS!

THE MILITARY IS DRAGGING ITS FEET. THEY THINK THESE REPORTS ARE JUST A HOAX.

WE DON'T NEED THEIR HELP TO HANDLE THIS MONSTER. WE HAVE RIFLES. WE CAN TAKE THEM OURSELVES AND TRACK DOWN--

RIFLES? *BAH!* MIGHT AS WELL THROW ROCKS AT THE THING.

WHO SAID THAT?

THAT WOULD BE ME...

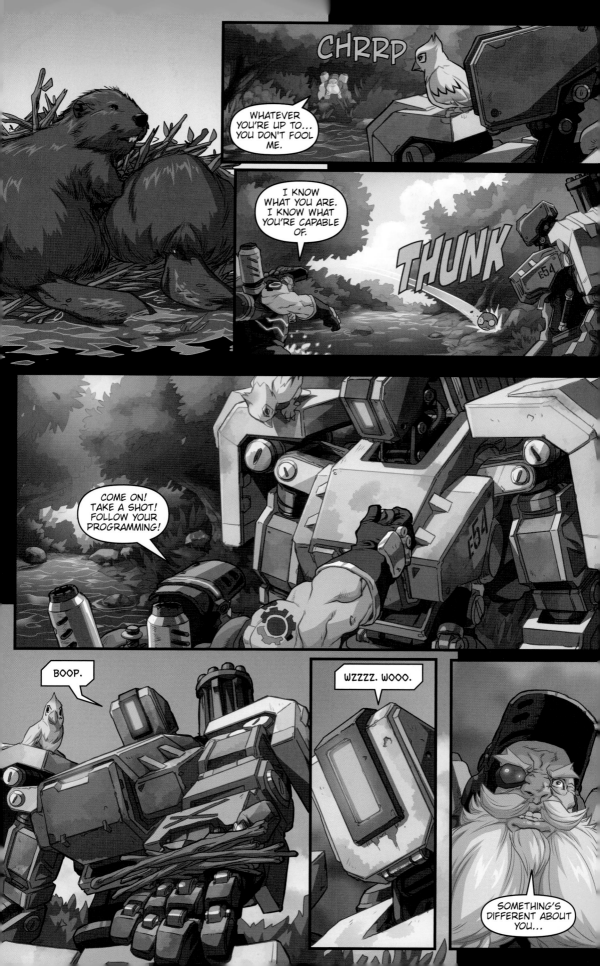

I'M ASKING YOU AS SOMEONE WHO'S SPENT MANY LONG YEARS FIGHTING THESE THINGS.

THIS BASTION IS DIFFERENT.

AND IF IT CAN CHANGE...

YOU REALLY HAVE LOST IT.

CALL OFF THE HUNT. I'M NOT GOING TO TELL YOU AGAIN.

RESTRAIN HIM!

CLIK

WATCH OUT!

CLINK

CLINK

CLINK

DON'T YOU HAVE ENOUGH BLOOD ON YOUR HANDS?

ENOUGH FOR A LIFETIME.

UPRISING

SCRIPT BY MICHAEL CHU | ART BY GRAY SHUKO

LETTERING BY RICHARD STARKINGS AND Comicraft's JOHN ROSHELL,

JIMMY BETANCOURT, AND ALBERT DESCHESNE

COME ON!

HOW IS SHE DOING?

UNFORTUNATELY, WE DON'T KNOW TOO MUCH ABOUT HER CONDITION.

BUT ASSUMING SHE DOESN'T EXPERIENCE ANY SETBACKS, I THINK SHE'S FIT FOR ACTIVE DUTY.

WE WILL NEED TO CONTINUE MONITORING HER TO SEE HOW SHE COPES.

TURNS OUT, TIME TRAVEL ISN'T AN EXACT SCIENCE. IS IT, WINSTON?

PROBLEMS?

NO!... WELL, NOTHING TOO SERIOUS... UH, SIR.

IN THE CONTEXT OF SOMEONE WHO CAN GET LOST IN TIME, WHAT DOES "NOTHING TOO SERIOUS" MEAN, WINSTON?

JUST A FEW RELIABILITY ISSUES TO WORK OUT, SIR.

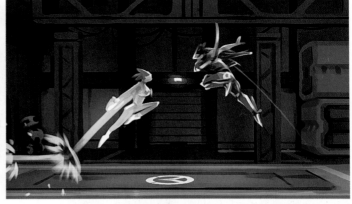

NOT BAD.

HAS THERE BEEN ANY UPDATE ON THE SITUATION IN LONDON, COMMANDER?

NOTHING GOOD. THE PRIME MINISTER HAS EXPRESSLY FORBIDDEN US FROM INTERVENING.

HE'S A FOOL, THEN. HOW MANY THOUSANDS IN KING'S ROW ARE IN NEED OF MEDICAL AID?

WHAT HAPPENS WHEN NULL SECTOR TAKES MORE OF THE CITY?

IT'LL BE EGYPT ALL OVER AGAIN, AND WE DON'T HAVE THE RESOURCES TO DEAL WITH ANOTHER HUMANITARIAN CRISIS.

THIS IS WHAT OVERWATCH WAS MADE FOR. INSTEAD OF WASTING TIME SITTING ON THE SIDELINES, WE COULD BE SAVING LIVES.

I DON'T DISAGREE, DOCTOR, BUT MY HANDS ARE TIED.

WELL, THAT'S NOT GOOD ENOUGH, JACK. AND A LOT OF PEOPLE ARE GOING TO DIE.

I KNOW, DR. ZIEGLER.

TELL OXTON I'D LIKE TO SPEAK WITH HER WHEN SHE'S FINISHED HERE.

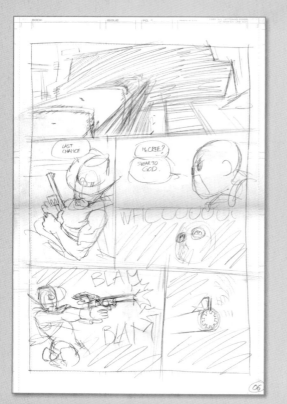

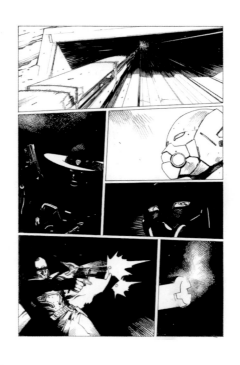

TOP LEFT

Rough concept for the cover.

TOP RIGHT

An early color pass on the

BOTTOM LEFT

Rough layout for page six.

BOTTOM RIGHT

The inked version of page six.

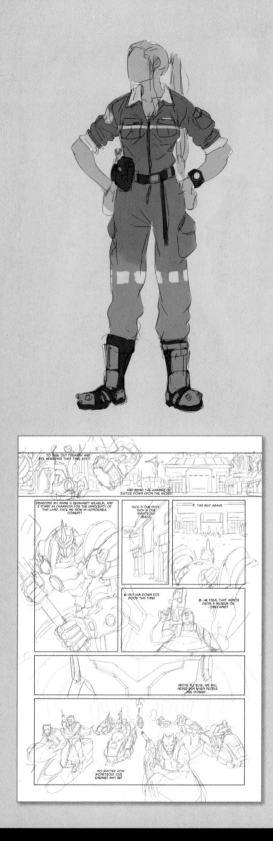

TOP LEFT

Early concept for Brigitte, Reinhardt's squire in "Dragon Slayer."

TOP RIGHT

Rough cover concept for "Dragon Slayer."

BOTTOM LEFT

Rough layout for page five of "Dragon Slayer."

BOTTOM RIGHT

Color pass of page five. Small adjustments were made between this version and the earlier layout, such as the design of the last panel.

cover thumbnails

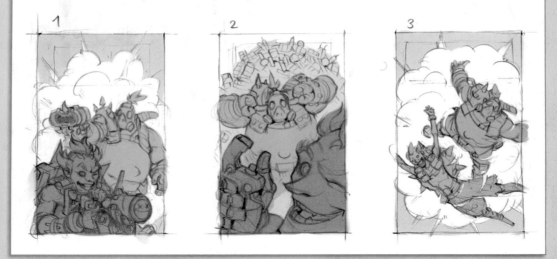

TOP LEFT

Rough layout for page five of "A Better World."

TOP RIGHT

Alternate cover concept of "A Better World" featuring

BOTTOM LEFT

Character concept for Khalil, one of Pharah's comrades in

BOTTOM RIGHT

An early cover concept for "Mission Statement." The

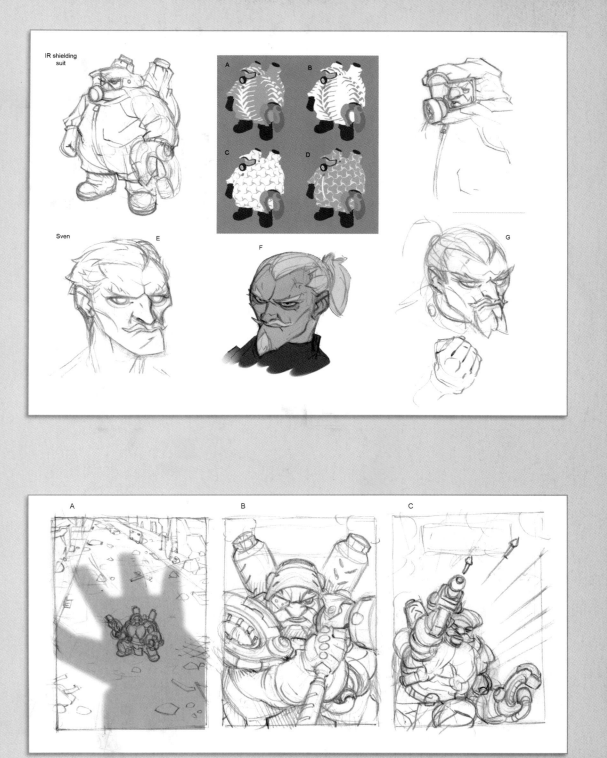

TOP

Concept art for Torbjörn's hazmat suit and Sven, the antagonist of "Destroyer."

BOTTOM

Cover concepts for "Destroyer." The creators chose the middle image for the final version.

TOP LEFT

Rough layout of page seven for "Legacy."

TOP RIGHT

Color version of page seven. The last panel was adjusted from the rough layout, and revealing the identity of Ana's foe—Amélie Lacroix, otherwise known as Widowmaker—was moved to the next page.

BOTTOM LEFT

Rough cover concept for "Old Soldiers."

BOTTOM RIGHT

Inked version of page four of "Old Soldiers."

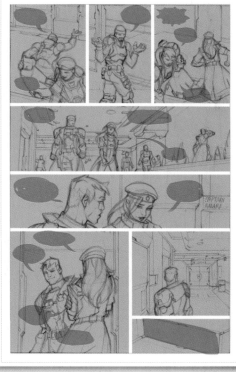

TOP LEFT

Rough cover concept for "Binary."

TOP RIGHT

Rough cover concept for "Binary." The creators ultimately chose a cover without Torbjörn to keep his appearance in the comic a surprise.

BOTTOM LEFT

Rough cover concept for "Uprising."

BOTTOM RIGHT

Rough layout for page three of "Uprising." Word balloons were added in this version to make sure they wouldn't be covering characters' faces or other important details.

RUSSIAN

ITALIAN

FRENCH

PORTUGUESE

JAPANESE

TRADITIONAL CHINESE

CREATOR BIOS

BENGAL—Bengal is best known for illustrating several popular European graphic novels, including *Meka*, *Naja*, and *Luminae*; for his recent work for DC Comics on *Batgirl* and *The Adventures of Supergirl*, the tie-in comic to the hit TV series *Supergirl*; and for his current *Spider-Gwen* and *All-New Wolverine* comics for Marvel. His unique style blends the dynamism of Japanese manga and anime with digital painting techniques from the fields of concept art and cover design.

ROBERT BROOKS—Robert Brooks is a senior writer on Blizzard's Creative Development team and has worked on content for all of the company's franchises. He recently co-authored the *New York Times* and *USA Today* bestselling illustrated history book series *World of Warcraft Chronicle*.

MATT BURNS—Matt Burns is a senior writer on Blizzard Entertainment's Creative Development team. During his time at the company, he has helped create licensed and ancillary fiction for the *World of Warcraft*, *StarCraft*, *Diablo*, and *Overwatch* universes. Some of his recent projects include authoring *Diablo III: Book of Tyrael* and co-authoring the *New York Times* and *USA Today* bestselling illustrated history book series *World of Warcraft Chronicle*.

MICHAEL CHU—Michael Chu is the lead writer for *Overwatch* at Blizzard Entertainment, where he began his career in 2000. He has worked on a number of other games, including *World of Warcraft*, *Diablo III*, and *Star Wars: Knights of the Old Republic II*.

JEFFREY "CHAMBA" CRUZ—Jeffrey "Chamba" Cruz is a Melbourne-based comic book artist whose credits include UDON's *Street Fighter II Turbo* series, *Super Street Fighter* volumes 1 and 2, *Skullkickers*, and *Wayward* from Image Comics.

Other properties and companies he's worked for include *Teenage Mutant Ninja Turtles*, Marvel, *Red Sonja*, Warner Bros., Mattel, Universal Pictures, *Mega Man*, DC Comics, IDW, BOOM! Studios, and Dynamite Entertainment.

Above all, his primary goal is to continue work on his original graphic novel *RandomVeus* (also published through UDON) and to continue creating and illustrating.

ESPEN GRUNDETJERN—Espen Grundetjern started his career in 2002 as a colorist on the *Transformers* comic series from Dreamwave Productions. Since 2005 he has colored primarily for UDON Entertainment on its *Street Fighter* and *Darkstalkers* series. Espen has also provided color illustration for video games such as *Tatsunoko vs. Capcom*, *Super Street Fighter II Turbo HD Remix*, and *Super Puzzle Fighter II Turbo HD Remix*, as well as working on concept art, promotional comics, and trading cards.

MIKI MONTLLÓ—Miki Montlló is an artist born in Barcelona and based in Ireland. He has worked in animation (Filmax, Cartoonsaloon, Laika) and comics for twelve years. He is currently working on the last books of his own science fiction saga, *Warship Jolly Roger*, published by Dargaud and Magnetic Press.

MICKY NEILSON—Micky Neilson worked at Blizzard Entertainment for twenty-two years, where his game-writing credits included *World of Warcraft*, *StarCraft*, *Warcraft III*, and *Lost Vikings 2*. Micky's first comic book, *World of Warcraft: Ashbringer*, hit #2 on the *New York Times* Best Sellers list for Hardcover Graphic Books. His graphic novel, *World of Warcraft: Pearl of Pandaria*, reached #3 on the *New York Times* Best Sellers list. In 2014, his *Diablo III* novella, *Morbed*, was published, as well as his long-awaited novella *Blood of the Highborne*. With the understanding support of his wife, Tiffany, and daughter, Tatiana, Micky looks forward to finding dark, quiet corners of the house to write in for years to come.

NESSKAIN—Born in 1987, Nesskain is a French comic artist residing near Paris. He started drawing around the end of high school, but he began to take it seriously around age twenty and spent all of his time practicing. He always desired to go to art school, so after getting a degree in engineering at twenty-two, he commenced his studies in comics, illustration, and animation—but left after six months. Mainly self-taught, he started working in the comics field the following year for the publisher Delcourt. His graphic novels include *Le Cercle* and *R.U.S.T.*.

JOE NG—Joe Ng is an illustrator from Toronto, Canada, and has worked on comics for *Transformers*, *G.I. Joe*, and *Street Fighter*. He has recently finished working on the twelve-issue *Street Fighter Unlimited* series for UDON Entertainment

ANDREW ROBINSON—Andrew Robinson has written and consulted for some thirty animated TV shows in the last sixteen years, including co-creating and overseeing the series *Kaijudo: Rise of the Duel Masters*, which ran two seasons. Lured by the incredible storytelling potential he saw in Blizzard's games, he joined the company at the end of 2014, and has been happily writing cinematic shorts and in-game content—and now comics—for its various intellectual properties since then.

GRAY SHUKO—A comics and concept artist, Gray Shuko has worked mainly for video game companies, in French studios, and at Blizzard. He is now a freelance artist focusing on PC and mobile games and on his new comic, *Fruity Frags*, which can be read on gray-shuko.net. Gray also spends time testing and upgrading his coloring technique, often by making fan art for two of his favorite franchises: *Dragon Ball Z* and *Metal Gear Solid*.

JAMES WAUGH—James Waugh is the former Senior Director of Story & Creative Development at Blizzard Entertainment, where he was instrumental in the development of the *Overwatch* universe, guiding the original slate of animated shorts, comics, and other media that helped introduce Blizzard's first new intellectual property in seventeen years. After eight years of developing the worlds of Azeroth, Sanctuary, and the Koprulu sector, he left Blizzard Entertainment in October 2016.

Currently Waugh serves as a Vice President of Development at Lucasfilm. Blizzard and its amazing universes (and amazing people) will always be near and dear to his heart.

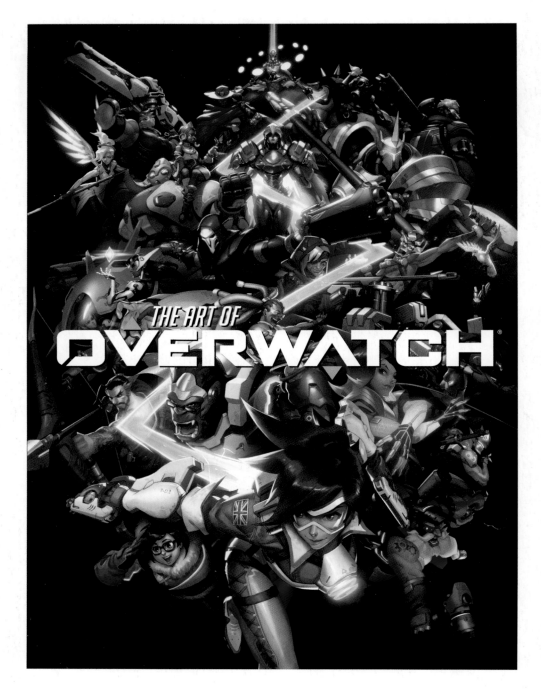